forest

doe

antlers

stag

leaves

fir-trees

conkers

fir-cones

violets

cowslips

butterfly

lily-of-the-valley

basket

rain

toadstool

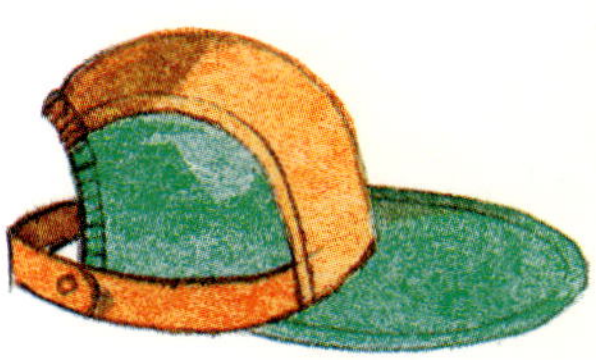

cap

Published in the UK in 1994 by Schofield & Sims Limited, Huddersfield, England.

0 7217 5021 4

PLAY WORDS

In the Forest

SCHOFIELD & SIMS LIMITED, HUDDERSFIELD, ENGLAND

wings

beak

eggs

nest

Birds 

Most  make their  in the trees. The mother  lays some 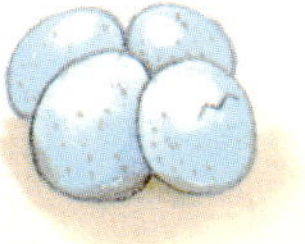 . Later on, the 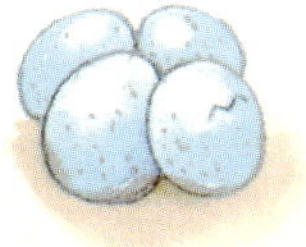 hatch. The chicks open their  wide to eat. Soon, the little  spread their  and fly away into the sky.

tail branch acrobat nuts

The squirrel 

The  is a little animal which can be red or grey. It has a big fluffy . The  is as quick and nimble as an . It climbs up trees and leaps from  to . The  loves eating berries, acorns and .

muzzle

lair

cub

hen

The fox 

The  has a bushy tail and a long, pointed  . It is a very cunning animal. At night, the  leaves its  to hunt. It has to feed its little  . The  catches rabbits, birds, mice and even  .

snout

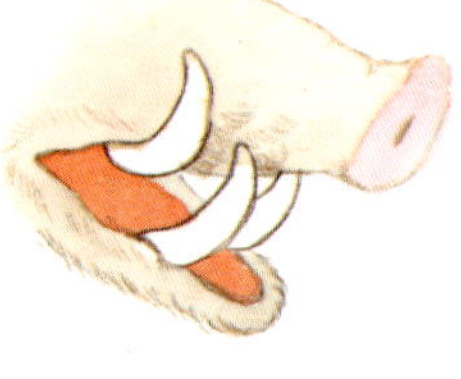

tusks

acorns

young boar

The boar 

The  is a wild pig with large 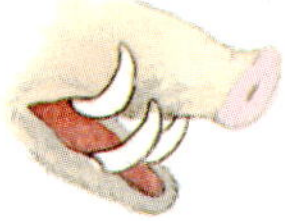 . Using its  , the  hunts on the ground to find  , which it loves. The skin of the  is light brown with darker stripes. The  love to run and play together.

forest

doe

antlers

stag

The fawn 

The little  is born in the spring. It loves to play in the middle of the . When it gets hungry, it suckles milk from its mother, the . The coat of a  is brown with white spots. Its father is the . He has huge  on his head.

leaves

fir-trees

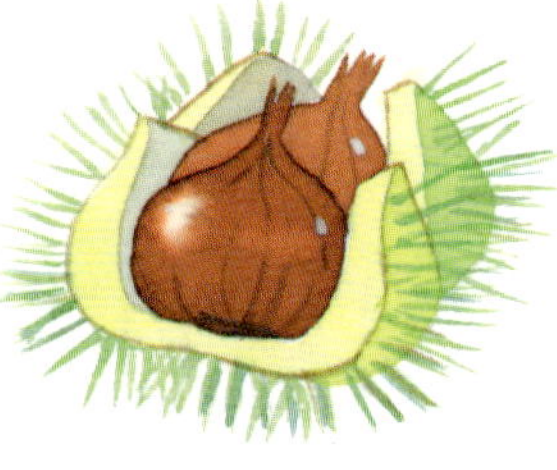

conkers

fir-cones

Trees 

In autumn, the  in the forest change colour. Their  turn golden, then fall to the ground. Only the  and the pine trees stay green. At the foot of the  you can find 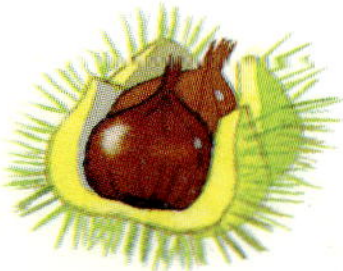 and . The trunks of the  are protected by bark.

violets

cowslips

butterfly

lily-of-the-valley

Flowers 

In the springtime, there are

 everywhere. Fields are full

of yellow daffodils and  .

We can also see  . Among the

 is the  , which is thought

to bring good luck. It has a beautiful

scent. The  loves to rest on

the  .

basket

rain

toadstool

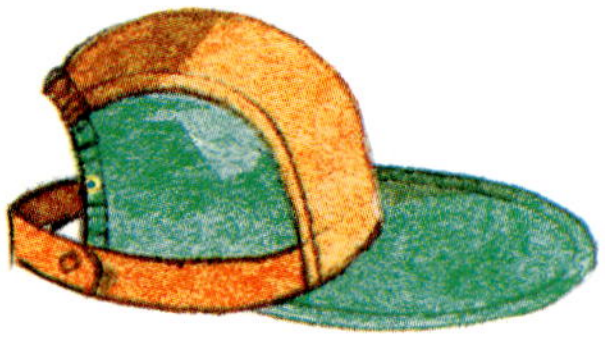

cap

Mushrooms 

After the  in autumn, we can find many . With your parents, you can fill up your . Be careful! – some  are poisonous, particularly those with a red and white . Mushrooms are fragile and should be picked carefully.

wings

beak

eggs

nest

tail

branch

acrobat

nuts

muzzle

lair

cub

hen

snout

tusks

acorns

young boar